CONTENTS

DATE DUE

FEB 10 '99

DISCARDED

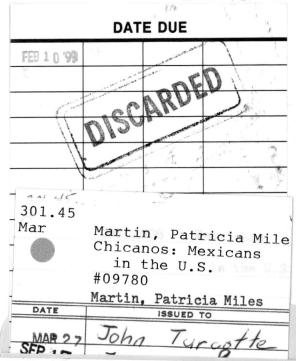

301.45
Mar

Martin, Patricia Mile
Chicanos: Mexicans
in the U.S.
#09780

Martin, Patricia Miles

DATE	ISSUED TO
MAR 27	John Turcotte
SEP 15	

301.45
Mar

Martin, Patricia Miles
Chicanos: Mexicans
in the United States
#09780

A Stepping-Stone Book

CHICANOS

Mexicans in the United States

by PATRICIA MILES MARTIN
Illustrated by ROBERT FRANKENBERG

Parents' Magazine Press · New York

Chapter 1
LONG AGO

Americans of Mexican descent call themselves Chicanos or Mexican Americans.

The great story of Mexican Americans begins long ago. Before Columbus came to the New World, Indians—the Mayas, the Toltecs, the Aztecs—had lived in Mexico for thousands of years. They built high stone pyramids that reached toward the sun, and it was there that the people honored their gods.

Later, the Indians built great and beautiful cities in Mexico. In their cities were palaces with walls of gold. There in the palaces the rulers held court.

Around the palaces were thousands of houses where workers lived—bakers, tailors, pottery makers, jewelers, artists.

Children went to school to study mathematics and art.

Beyond the cities, farmers lived in small villages and farmed the land around them. They grew cotton and corn, squash, chili peppers, and beans. They wove cotton into cloth to make their clothes, and they ground corn into meal to make their bread.

They learned the story of their beginnings—a
story that the old ones had written on deerskin
and on paper made from the bark of the wild
fig tree:

Long ago,
in a time that is
almost forgotten,
our forefathers who
came first,
came over the sea,
came over the deep water
in boats made of rushes.
They carried baskets
of earth
and filled the marshes
and made the land .good.
Then they chose men to lead us,
men to rule over our land.

These were the leaders for hundreds of years,
until Spanish explorers landed on the shores of

Mexico. The Spaniards came with cannon and gunpowder and horses to use in battle.

The people of Mexico had never seen horses. They knew only the wild things of their own land—jaguars, bears, deer. They had never heard the blast of gunpowder.

The Spaniards galloped into battle. Their guns blasted. Their cannon roared. And soon they overcame millions of brave Indians who fought only with spears, bows and arrows, and clubs.

The great cities were destroyed. Many villages were taken from the farmers. These villages and the families who lived in them were given to Spanish soldiers.

Spain ruled the land for three hundred years. During all those years, Spanish men married Indian women, and their children spoke the language of Spain. These children of Spanish and Indian peoples called themselves *Mestizos,* which means "mixed."

And during most of this time, Spanish explorers searched for more land. They set out from Mexico and traveled to the north. They found land that is now part of the United States.

This was Indian land, but the Spaniards claimed it for Spain. It became a Spanish colony. To settle the new colony, the government sent packtrains to the north. The priests, called *padres,* led the way along the king's highway,

El Camino Real. They took with them patient burros loaded with supplies for the packtrains. They also carried presents for the Indians in the north. Spanish and *mestizo* soldiers and settlers followed where the *padres* led. The soldiers built forts, and the settlers built little huts clustered together in small villages.

Thousands of friendly Indians took the
presents that were given to them. In return for
food and shelter, the Indians helped build
churches, schools, and other buildings. These
groups of buildings were called missions.

The *padres* taught them the language and religion of Spain. The Indians lived in the missions and worked in the fields to raise food so everyone could eat. They herded the horses and cattle that roamed in wide pastures. But they were forced to stay and work in the missions as long as they lived.

Near each mission, the soldiers built a fort to

protect the *padres,* for there were other Indians in the colony who fought to keep their land.

Wherever they chose, the Spanish government took Indian lands in the new colony, as they had done in Mexico. The Spanish government gave this land in the new colony to their friends in high office. Many grants of land covered miles and miles of beautiful valleys and forests.

Chapter 2
TIME OF TROUBLE

In Mexico, the farmers worked in fields and lived in villages that once belonged to their own Indian forefathers, land that had been taken by the Spanish government. Now the farmers worked for others.

They still raised corn and squash, chili peppers and beans. But they had to give a large part of the crops they raised to the owners of the land.

On September 16, 1810, the angry people from the fields banded together to fight for their land.

After years of bitter fighting, the Spanish rulers from across the sea were overthrown. A new government was formed, called the United Mexican States.

After the Spanish government was overthrown, farmers still fought for their land, for men in high office in the new government wanted their land. Also, men in the government of the United States wanted land. They wanted the colony that lay north of Mexico.

Mexicans fought to keep it, but the weaker nation lost to the stronger, and the colony became part of the United States of America. Later this colony became the states of Texas, New Mexico, Utah, Arizona, California, and a part of Colorado.

When the war was over a treaty was made between the two countries. The United States promised that all Mexicans who owned land in the United States could stay and keep their lands. If they wished, they could become United States citizens.

Those who stayed became citizens, but often they were not able to keep their lands.

Sometimes they could not find the old papers they needed to prove that land grants had been made to their families. Others did not know the English language and were tricked into signing papers that gave their land to strangers.

In Mexico, revolution followed revolution.

During the time of trouble, many Mexicans came across the Rio Grande with their families,

hoping to find peace in the United States.

Many came only to work in the summers, but some came to stay. Many of those who stayed became citizens of the United States.

But whether they became citizens, or whether they returned to Mexico after a summer's work, all of their children who were born north of the Mexican border were citizens of the United States.

Each man who came to the United States had to have a pass from the Mexican government. The United States patrol watched the border between the two countries, to see that those without passes did not cross the river.

Even so, families who had no passes often came to the United States. They came secretly in the night.

In the dry season, when the river was low, they waded across. From May to October, in the time of the rains, when the river ran high, they came on rafts or on strange boats called ducks. The ducks were made of dried willow branches tied together with ropes, and each one could carry twelve people.

The Mexicans who came secretly had to find shelter. As soon as they arrived, they looked for branches and twigs to make a little shelter in the brush. They covered the shelter with leaves and mud until it looked like a part of the earth, hidden from the patrol that would send them back to Mexico if they were found.

Chapter 3
WORKERS

Today, many still cross the river in secret, hoping to find relatives or friends who will give them a place to live and help them find work. But most Mexicans get their passes and cross the bridge over the Rio Grande with their families.

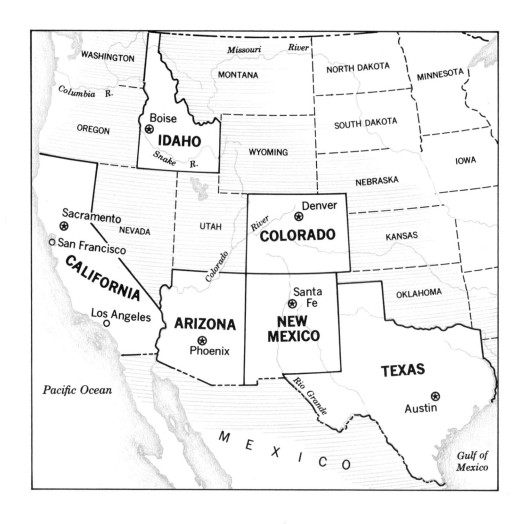

Mexicans work and live all over the United States, especially in Texas, New Mexico, California, Idaho, Colorado, and Arizona—the West and Southwest of the United States—but also in many other states.

Those with special skills work in the cities. Some are teachers, some are doctors. Others work in stores or in factories. Many work on the railroads.

But workers usually come to work on the farms and ranches. If they have no cars, buses meet them at the border and take them to farms where their work is needed.

In the early spring, the farm workers pick the crops that are ready for harvest.

In a lettuce field, mother, father, and the older boys and girls work all day, cutting each head of lettuce from its root. If the grower will let them, children as young as nine years old help, too.

These are the migrant workers, men who go
from farm to farm, following the harvesting
time of the crops.

In the late spring, the workers go to another
farm. In the summer, they pick strawberries and
other crops. In the fall, they pick grapes in the
vineyards.

Most families live on the farms where they work.

On a small farm, perhaps twelve families are needed.

On one such farm, the workers live in twelve small tumbledown shacks. The windows are boarded over. There is no running water in the houses. The children carry water from a well.

On a large farm, as many as seventy-five families may live in a row of rooms built of cement blocks. Each family has one room. Inside the rooms are running water and electricity.

Other families live together in camps within driving distance of the farms where they work. These may be five miles or fifty miles from their camp.

Chapter 4
MIGRANT WORKERS' CAMP

The government has helped build camps where some of the migrant workers live.

In such a camp, one hundred families live in small houses, one to a family.

The family is a close family, each working to

help the other. The mother and father speak
Spanish to their children, for they want them to
remember the language of Mexico.

The woman of the family fixes supper on a
small electric stove. And in a separate building
there are washing machines where she may
wash the clothes her family wears.

These plain little houses—pink, yellow, gray
—are built around a great central square, where
grass struggles to grow and a few young trees
reach toward the sun.

In the morning, the workers in families
climb into their cars and drive away. The

smaller children are left at home. Sometimes the younger children stay with a grandmother or an older sister. If there is no one in the family to watch over them, the younger ones may be left in a Child Care Center at the camp.

Young children learn a few words of English in the Center. A mother who speaks both Spanish and English is the teacher.

The children learn the ABC's—A for Ant, B for Balloon, C for Cactus . . .

Children too young to learn their ABC's beat out music on triangles, drums, or *maracas,* dried gourds with rattling seeds inside.

Mexican mothers at the Child Care Center fix food that their children like—chili beans, *tortillas,* which are flat corn cakes, and green salads.

When it is time for the older children to go to school, school buses stop at farms and camps.

Children of migrant workers can go to one particular school only as long as their parents work in the nearby fields. When a crop has been harvested and the father moves on to find another place to work, his family goes with him, and the children go to another school.

Older boys and girls have gone to many schools over the years, as their parents followed the harvest seasons of the different crops.

After the harvests are over, the farm worker puts his belongings in the back of his car. His family crowds into the car, happy to be on the way home.

Some men take their families back to their small *pueblos,* or villages, in Mexico. Many migrant workers return to their own *barrios,* or neighborhoods, in the United States.

Chapter 5
NEIGHBORHOODS

Many Mexican Americans live in their own *barrios,* or neighborhoods, in the United States.

When Mexicans first came to the United States, they lived where they found other Mexican families, where rent was cheapest, where they could talk the language of home. And so it happened that they lived close together—brothers near brothers, friends near friends.

In the valley of the Rio Grande, the little houses on the United States side are much like the houses just across the river in Mexico. The houses have floors of hard-packed earth. There is no electricity or running water inside.

Across the nation, there are huge *barrios* in large cities, such as El Paso, Chicago, Denver, Los Angeles.

The *barrios* on the east side of Los Angeles make up the third largest Mexican city in the world. Chicanos live at the edge of the city that was once the *Pueblo* of Los Angeles, founded by their own forefathers.

In other cities there are smaller

neighborhoods, where thousands of Chicanos live.

In such a neighborhood, at the edge of San Jose, in California, a long street marks the boundary between the Chicano neighborhood and the rest of the city.

On the Chicano side, there are used car lots and filling stations. There are also stores of all kinds along the quiet street.

Inside one grocery store are great baskets of dried chili peppers and beans. There are pottery bowls and toys from Mexico. There are *piñatas* —huge pottery and paper-covered roosters and ducks. These are filled with candies. Children with blindfolds over their eyes break them in the *Piñata* game, played on their days of celebration.

There are fresh *tortillas* in plastic packages.
The *tortillas* are made in a kitchen at the
back of the store.

In a drug store, boys and girls find the
records they like best, made by Chicano singers
and bands. They find books printed in Spanish.

Some of the men in the neighborhood are farm workers who drive to nearby farms in the morning and come back again at night. Others find work in the city, in stores and in factories.

Beyond the main street are the houses. The houses are small, but each has its own front yard, its little fence.

In some blocks, rose trees bloom in front yards. In other blocks, corn grows high in back yards.

Boys walk arm in arm along the street. Girls take care of small brothers and sisters.

The people of this neighborhood listen to Spanish music over their radios and they read the news in their Spanish newspapers.

They read about the *fiestas,* the celebrations of their forefathers. Weeks before each September sixteenth, Spanish newspapers and radios tell of plans for the *fiesta* celebrating the

day when the workers from the fields rose up
against their Spanish rulers.

At the *fiesta,* a Mexican flag and an American

flag are carried side by side at the head of a long parade.

Boys are dressed like *vacqueros,* or cowboys. Many boys and girls are in Mexican dress.

Women take food to the picnic grounds: platters of chicken or beef stew, pots of chili beans, and big bowls of green salads. There is food for everyone.

Music blasts over a loud speaker. There are speeches and dancing, laughing and singing.

This *fiesta* is a glorious time for all young Americans of Mexican descent.

Chapter 6
THE SCHOOLS

In schools across the nation, there are millions of American boys and girls of Mexican descent.

Many small children have been taught English as well as Spanish by their mothers and fathers. Others know only Spanish when they first go to school.

On that first day in school, when a boy and girl who know only Spanish open their reader, the English words have no meaning for them. Too often there is no one who can tell them what the words mean. Often the teacher and the other children in the classroom do not know the Spanish language.

In school, the boy and girl who speak only

Spanish can't learn their lessons, for they must understand English first of all. And so it happens that many smart boys and girls are kept in one grade until they know enough English to be able to read their lessons.

But the young Chicanos know many things that other children may not know.

They know about the fields of growing things.

They know about the vineyards where the grapes grow.

Boys know how to play soccer, one of the most popular games in the world today. They know that soccer was played before the game of football was invented, that two teams play with a round ball and players kick the ball or bat it with their heads.

Spanish-speaking young Americans feel pride in the Spanish language. When they speak English also, they can be twice proud, for they are then bilingual, speaking two languages.

In school, they learn about the Indians who were first in the United States. But nowhere in American history books do they find the full, proud story of their own great Mayas, Toltecs, and Aztecs of Mexico.

Those who finish their education do the work they want to do.

Chapter 7
FOR THE GOOD OF ALL

Mexican Americans work for the good of all people in the United States.

They are doctors and lawyers, newspaper editors and television broadcasters. Many are artists and writers. Others teach in colleges.

Chicanos are among the great players of baseball, football, tennis, and soccer. They are the finest horsemen in the world. The famous actor Anthony Quinn is a Mexican American.

The name of Cesar Chavez will be remembered as that of a Chicano who helped the farm workers. Once a migrant worker

himself, he knew they received too little pay for their hard labor. He asked the grape growers to meet and talk about higher pay. When all the grape growers could not agree, Chavez called the workers from the vineyards.

This was *la huelga*, the rest from work, a time when workers would not go to the vineyards. This was a strike.

57

Cesar Chavez asked all the people of the United States to stop buying grapes for their tables.

After a few years, the grape growers agreed to pay higher wages to the farm workers. And the workers went back to the fields.

Many other Mexican Americans all across the United States are now working for the good of their people.

Many people in the field of education work for the good of all young Spanish-speaking boys and girls. In vacation time, teachers teach in summer schools, which are open to children who need to learn English.

In Texas there are schools for children of kindergarten age. Small boys and girls learn four hundred words they will need to know in the first grade of school.

In the state of Washington, a school is open each summer for boys and girls of all ages who want to learn English.

When California became a state, many
Spanish-speaking leaders were among those who
made its first laws. California was made a
bilingual state, and schools were taught in
Spanish and in English. But in 1878, Spanish-
speaking leaders were pushed into the

background and Spanish was no longer spoken in the schools. Then for many years teachers taught their classes only in English, for this was the law of the state.

A few years ago, the law was changed, and classes may now be taught in Spanish as well as in English. This is also the law in other states, where many Chicano children go to school.

* * *

Mexican Americans have given many things to the United States.

Their forefathers discovered trails across the Southwest—trails that later became highways and rail lines.

They brought packtrains of burros and mules that carried supplies and mail over the trails for three hundred years before the coming of the railroads.

They helped to build the railroad lines.

In Texas, they cleared the desert land of brush. By hand they pulled out thickets and thorns, rat-tail cactus and greasewood, to make the pastures, fields, and gardens that are there today.

The quick growth of farms and factories all over the Southwest was made possible by their labor.

To the English language they added many new words. Ranch, rodeo, coyote, tornado, and chocolate are all Spanish words, brought with them from Mexico.

They gave their special music and dance.

They shared their weaving, perhaps the most

beautiful in the world. They shared their
other arts in bold paintings, in lacy tin work, in
fine silver work.

Some are in the Congress of the United
States, where they work for the good of all
people.

Americans of Mexican descent are a great
and important part of the United States of
America.

INDEX

63

CONNECTICUT
STATE DEPARTMENT OF EDUCATION
Bureau Of Elementary And Secondary Education
HARTFORD, CONNECTICUT